SPI

GOLF

ADVENTURES

Published by
Specks Golf Adventures
P.O. Box 20765
Sedona, AZ 86341

Preassigned LCCN: 97-78398
ISBN 1-886966-12-5

Manufactured in the United States of America
0 9 8 7 6 5 4 3 2 1

DEDICATION

This book is dedicated...

To the sheer joy, fun and camaraderie of golf.

To my wife, who said if I didn't she wouldn't do my laundry.

To tomorrow's golfers—the new youth of the game.

4

5

6

8

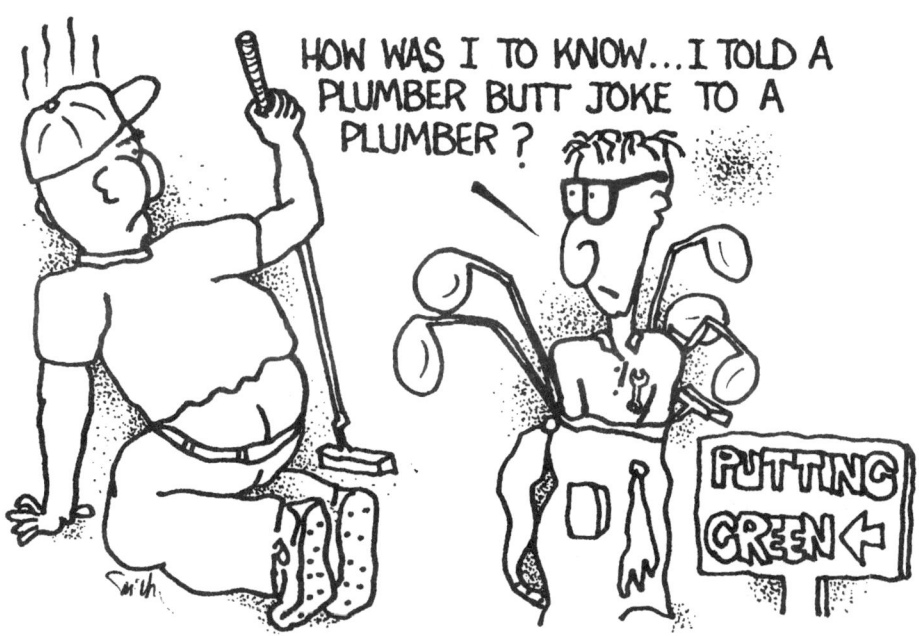

9

14

16

19

21

22

23

24

25

34

40

42

GOLF EXPECTATIONS ARE THE GREATEST OF ALL

44

45

46

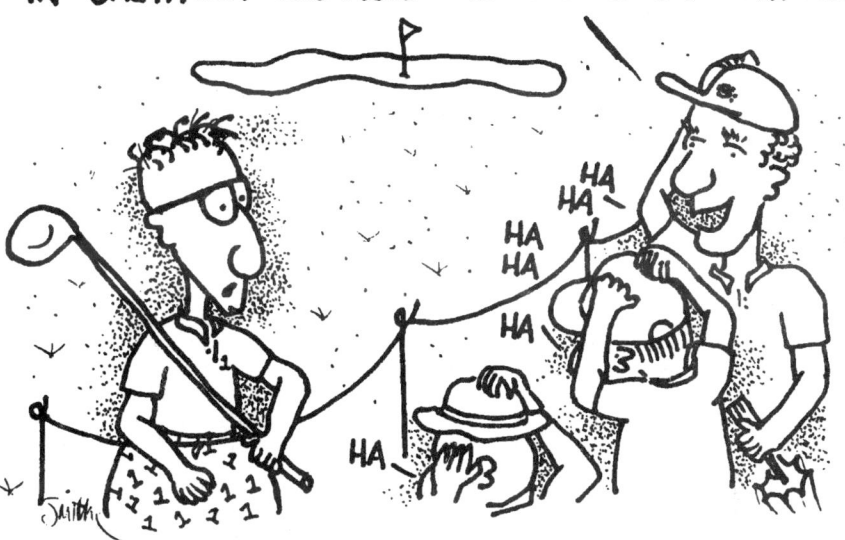

49

50

51

53

54

56

57

60

61

64

66

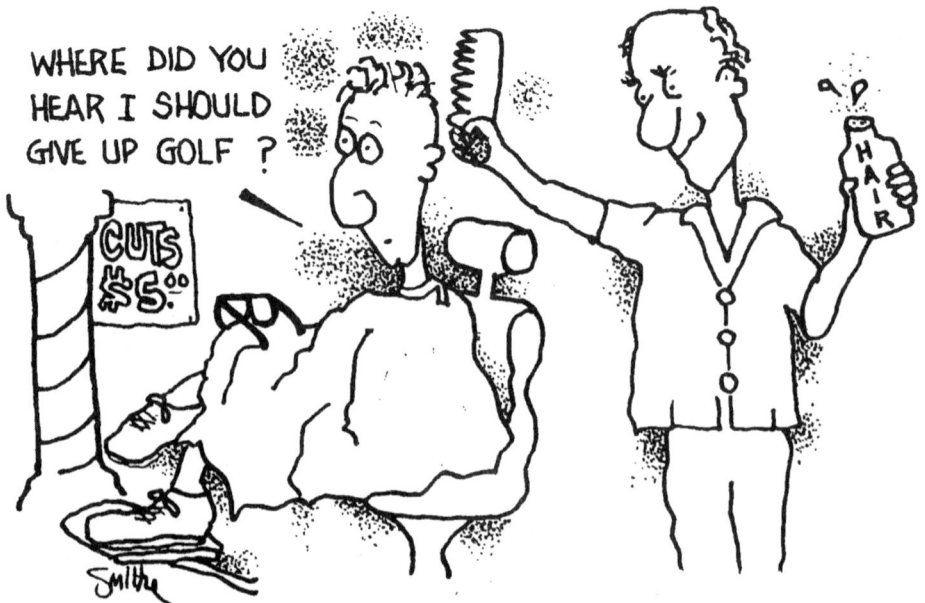

68

69

ATTENTION EVERYONE...ONLY TWO SPOTS REMAINING....
GOLF with CENTERFOLDS
TICKETS
PLAYMATE CENTERFOLDS ARE YOUR PARTNER
Smith

73

74

75

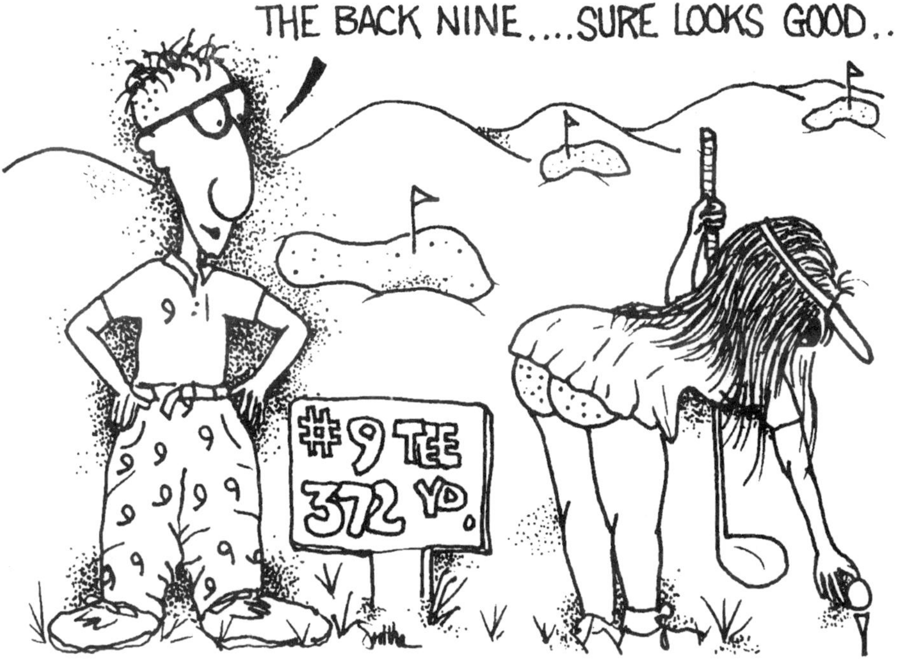
THE BACK NINE....SURE LOOKS GOOD..
#9 TEE
372 YD.

82

83

84

85

87

88

92

94

THE WAY HE FEELS ABOUT HIS CLUBS IS X-RATED

95

97

98

99

100

A LITTLE RAIN NEVER STOPPED US FROM IGNORING THE LUNCH HORN.

105

111

113

117

119

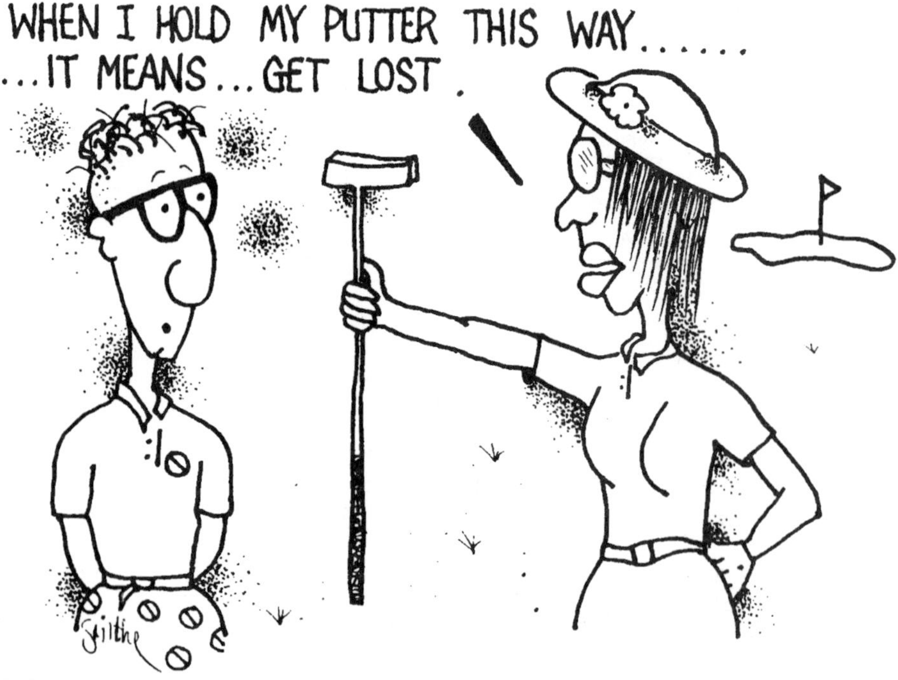
WHEN I HOLD MY PUTTER THIS WAY.......
...IT MEANS...GET LOST.

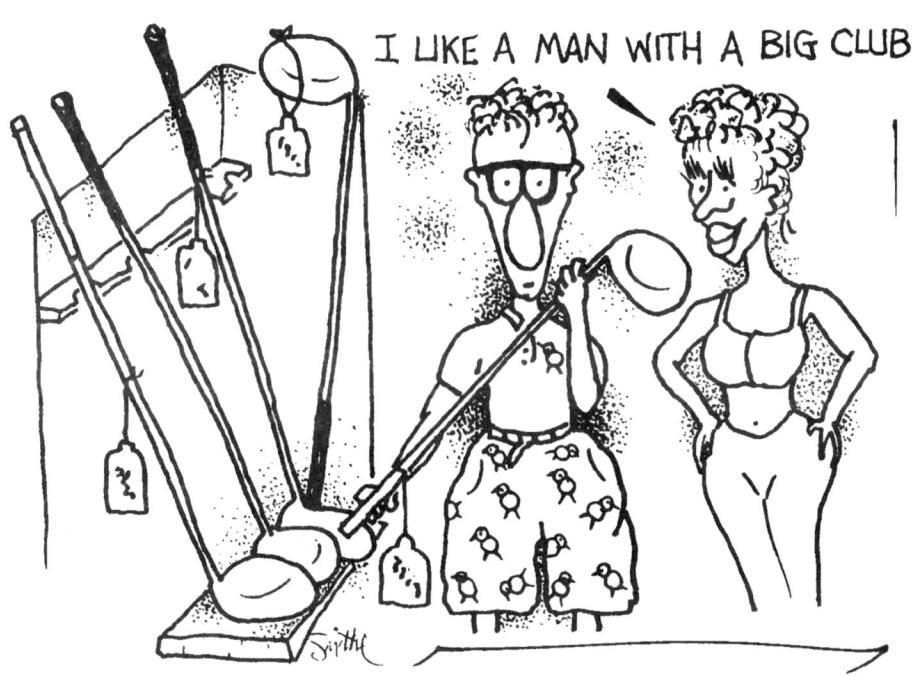

124